IF SATAN CAN'T STEAL YOUR JOY STUDY MANUAL

JERRY SAVELLE

Copyright 2024–Harrison House

All rights reserved. This book is protected by the copyright laws of the United States of America. This book may not be copied or reprinted for commercial gain or profit. The use of short quotations or occasional page copying for personal or group study is permitted and encouraged. Permission will be granted upon request. Unless otherwise indicated, all scripture quotations are taken from the *King James Version* of the Bible. Used by permission. All rights reserved.

All emphasis within Scripture quotations is the author's own. Please note that Harrison House's publishing style capitalizes certain pronouns in Scripture that refer to the Father, Son, and Holy Spirit, and may differ from some publishers' styles. Take note that the name satan and related names are not capitalized. We choose not to acknowledge him, even to the point of violating grammatical rules.

Harrison House P.O. Box 310, Shippensburg, PA 17257-0310

This book and all other Harrison House's books are available at Christian bookstores and distributors worldwide.

Reach us on the Internet: www.harrisonhouse.com.

ISBN 13 TP: 9781667510705

ISBN 13 eBook: 9781667510712

Contents

1. ...He Can't Keep Your Goods — 1
2. ...He Can't Defeat You — 9
3. ...He Can't Deceive You — 17
4. Satan Targets Your Dreams — 25
5. It's Time to Recapture Your Dreams — 33

About the Author — 39
About the Publisher — 41

Chapter 1

...He Can't Keep Your Goods

"The thief does not come except to steal, and to kill, and to destroy. I have come that they may have life, and that they may have it more abundantly." (John 10:10, NKJV)

It was a day that should have been just another step in the journey of faith, but instead, it turned into a trial that tested every word Jerry Savelle had believed. His car—a 1964 Oldsmobile 98—was his faithful companion through years of ministry preparation, even though it had seen better days. That morning, as he shared his testimony of God's provision with a former employer, something unexpected happened. Just as he started his engine to leave, the car exploded in flames right in front of him. In that moment, everything he had been confessing about God's abundance and faithfulness was put on trial. Would he still believe in prosperity now that his last means of transportation was nothing but smoldering wreckage?

That moment became a defining lesson about the tactics of the enemy. The devil is not interested in attacking what has no value. He targets what God has given, seeking to steal joy, faith, and provision from believers. The enemy's goal is always the same—to make Christians doubt God's Word, to rob them of confidence, and ultimately to strip them of the spiritual and material blessings meant for them.

But as Jerry Savelle would soon discover, faith in God's promises does not crumble under attacks—it is meant to stand firm. The enemy may come to steal, but he cannot keep what rightfully belongs to a child of God. The car may have been destroyed, but the principle of supernatural provision remained intact.

The question then is not whether Satan will try to steal from us—he will. The real question is, will we allow him to keep what he has stolen? Or will we rise up, stand firm in faith, and demand the return of everything that belongs to us?

Focus Point

"Resist the devil and he will flee from you." (James 4:7, NKJV)

This verse is a declaration of spiritual authority. Satan does not have unlimited power over believers—he operates through deception and intimidation. When a Christian recognizes the enemy's schemes and actively resists him through faith, prayer, and declaration of God's Word, the enemy has no choice but to flee. This is not a passive stance but an active one, requiring believers to stand in their rightful authority and refuse to let Satan keep what he has unlawfully taken.

Main Theme

The central theme of this chapter is the undeniable authority believers have over Satan's theft. The devil's nature is that of a thief, and he targets joy, peace, finances, health, and faith in an attempt to rob God's people of their abundant life. However, as seen throughout Scripture, the righteous are not defenseless. God has provided His Word as a weapon, and joy as strength. Faith is the mechanism that retrieves stolen blessings, and perseverance in the face of trials leads to supernatural restoration.

"If Satan can't steal your joy, he can't keep your goods."

Key Scriptures

- *"Behold, I give you the authority to trample on serpents and scorpions, and over all the power of the enemy, and nothing shall by any means hurt you."* (Luke 10:19, NKJV)
- *"But the path of the just is like the shining sun, that shines ever brighter unto the perfect day."* (Proverbs 4:18, NKJV)
- *"The Lord shall fight for you, and you shall hold your peace."* (Exodus 14:14, NKJV)

Key Points

- **Satan's Primary Goal Is to Steal** The enemy is a thief by nature. He does not come for any reason but to steal, kill, and destroy. His primary focus is on stealing the Word of God from believers' hearts because he knows that faith comes by hearing and receiving the Word.
- **Healing Is Already Yours** Many believers struggle with healing because they see it as something they need to attain rather than something they already possess. Healing is not something distant; it is an inheritance secured through Christ. The enemy's goal is not to give sickness but to steal divine health.
- **You Are Not Trying to Get Victory—You Have It** Just as a thief cannot legally take what already belongs to another, Satan has no right to hold on to the blessings of a believer. Victory is already secured in Christ, and faith is the legal claim that enforces its reality.
- **Satan Comes to Steal the Word First** When the Word of God is received, the enemy immediately seeks to snatch it away through distractions, trials, or hardships. This is why so many believers experience increased opposition after receiving a revelation—Satan is attempting to prevent it from taking root.
- **Joy Is a Weapon Against the Enemy** The joy of the Lord is not just a feeling—it is strength (Nehemiah 8:10). Joy is a force that keeps believers resilient in the face of trials. If Satan can steal joy, he weakens faith, but when joy remains, faith remains strong.
- **You Have a Right to Demand Restoration** Proverbs 6:31 states that when a thief is caught, he must restore sevenfold. This is a principle believers can stand on: whatever has been stolen must be returned, and with interest.
- **Praise and Thanksgiving Break the Enemy's Hold** When facing trials, choosing to praise and give thanks is an act of faith that disrupts the enemy's strategy. Praise shifts focus from loss to God's ability to restore.

Journaling Questions

Journaling about the truths in this chapter is essential for developing a steadfast faith that refuses to let the enemy hold onto stolen blessings. Writing down past victories and answered prayers strengthens the believer's confidence in God's ability to restore. When believers document their experiences of resisting the enemy, it builds a personal testimony of overcoming through joy and faith.

Through journaling, readers will recognize patterns in their spiritual walk, identify areas where they need to stand firmer in faith, and develop a deeper awareness of how joy plays a role in reclaiming stolen blessings.

Recognizing the Thief

What are some areas in my life where Satan has attempted to steal my joy or blessings?

_____
_____
_____
_____
_____
_____
_____

Standing in Faith

How can I actively resist the enemy's attempts to steal my joy and possessions?

_____
_____
_____
_____
_____
_____
_____

Joy as a Weapon

When have I experienced supernatural strength through joy in difficult times?

Declaring Victory

What Scripture can I declare over my life to reinforce my faith against the enemy's attacks?

Expecting Restoration

In what specific ways am I believing for a sevenfold return of what the enemy has stolen?

Actionable Steps

Cultivate Joy in Every Season
Joy is not dependent on circumstances but on trust in God. Practice daily gratitude and laughter, even in trials, to strengthen faith.

Equip Yourself with the Word
The enemy cannot keep what you refuse to let go of. Meditate on and declare key Scriptures about restoration and divine protection.

Engage in Bold Faith Declarations
Speak over your life what God's Word declares—especially in the face of trials. Faith-filled words enforce spiritual authority.

Personal Reflection

There is a reason the enemy fights so hard to steal from you—he knows what you possess. Every trial, every moment of loss, is an attempt to weaken your faith and rob you of the abundant life God has promised. But as long as you refuse to surrender your joy, he cannot win.

Standing firm in faith requires intentionality. It means waking up every day and choosing to declare what God has spoken rather than what circumstances suggest. It means refusing to accept loss as final and believing in supernatural restoration. Faith is not passive; it is a declaration of victory in the face of opposition.

What are you refusing to let the enemy keep? What has been stolen that you are demanding to be restored? How will you stand in faith until you see God's promise fulfilled?

_____
_____
_____
_____
_____
_____
_____
_____
_____

Closing Prayer: Lord Jesus,

I refuse to allow the enemy to steal what You have given me. I stand in faith, declaring that every blessing, every promise, and every provision is secure in Your hands. I receive joy as my strength and restoration as my inheritance. Let my life be a testimony of Your faithfulness. In Jesus' name, Amen.

Chapter 2

...He Can't Defeat You

"No weapon formed against you shall prosper, and every tongue which rises against you in judgment You shall condemn. This is the heritage of the servants of the Lord, and their righteousness is from Me," says the Lord." (Isaiah 54:17, NKJV)

There was a time when Jerry Savelle felt completely outmatched. Early in his ministry, he found himself facing trials that seemed impossible to overcome. Financial difficulties, opposition, and self-doubt all came against him like a flood. One day, after what felt like endless resistance, he cried out to God, "Why is everything going wrong?" At that moment, God revealed a powerful truth: the devil doesn't fight against those who are not a threat—he only attacks those carrying a divine purpose.

This truth is the foundation of spiritual warfare. The enemy's attacks are not random; they are intentional. He targets believers who are walking in their God-given assignment because he knows that they carry the power to disrupt his kingdom. However, Satan is already a defeated foe. His only strategy is deception—making believers think they have lost when, in reality, victory is already theirs in Christ.

Understanding this changes everything. It removes fear and discouragement because no matter how fierce the battle, the outcome is already determined. The enemy may attack, but he cannot win. Every believer who stands firm in faith and refuses to be moved by circumstances will see the manifestation of God's promises.

The question is not whether the enemy will try to fight against you—he will. The real question is, will you allow temporary setbacks to convince you that you are defeated, or will you stand on the truth that you are already victorious in Christ?

Focus Point

"Yet in all these things we are more than conquerors through Him who loved us." (Romans 8:37, NKJV)

This verse is a declaration of absolute victory. It does not say that believers will barely overcome or simply survive attacks—it says that we are more than conquerors. This means that every challenge the enemy throws is not just meant to be defeated but turned into a testimony of God's power and faithfulness. Satan does not have the ability to defeat a believer who walks in this truth, because their victory is not based on their strength but on the finished work of Christ.

Main Theme

The central theme of this chapter is the believer's undefeatable position in Christ. Every spiritual battle has already been won through Jesus' victory on the cross. The enemy's attacks are designed to deceive believers into surrendering their authority, but those who stand firm in faith will always see triumph. No matter how many weapons are formed against a child of God, they cannot prosper.

"Victory is not something you fight for—it is something you enforce."

Key Scriptures

- *"Thanks be to God, who gives us the victory through our Lord Jesus Christ."* (1 Corinthians 15:57, NKJV)
- *"For whatever is born of God overcomes the world. And this is the victory that has overcome the world—our faith."* (1 John 5:4, NKJV)
- *"The Lord will cause your enemies who rise against you to be defeated before your face; they shall come out against you one way and flee before you seven ways."* (Deuteronomy 28:7, NKJV)

Key Points

- **Satan Can Only Defeat Those Who Surrender** The enemy has no power except what a believer gives him through fear, doubt, and unbelief. Victory is maintained by refusing to surrender to his lies.
- **Faith is the Victory** Victory is not about external circumstances—it is about maintaining faith in God's promises. Faith is what enforces the victory that has already been won.
- **Opposition is Proof of Destiny** The size of the attack often indicates the size of the calling. The enemy does not waste time attacking those who are not a threat to his kingdom.
- **The Word of God is Your Weapon** Jesus defeated Satan in the wilderness by declaring the Word. Likewise, believers must use Scripture as a weapon against every lie of the enemy.
- **Fear is the Enemy's Open Door** Fear allows the enemy access to a believer's mind. Faith shuts that door and keeps him out.
- **Victory is a Mindset Before It is a Reality** Those who think in terms of defeat will live in defeat. Those who renew their minds to think in terms of victory will walk in victory.
- **Praise Secures the Victory** Paul and Silas praised God in prison before their breakthrough. Worship is an act of faith that enforces the enemy's defeat.

Journaling Questions

Journaling about the truths in this chapter allows believers to document their journey of overcoming opposition. Writing down personal victories, past deliverances, and testimonies of God's faithfulness strengthens faith in times of battle.

By reflecting on these truths, believers will begin to recognize patterns in the enemy's attacks and develop strategies to stand firm against them. This section serves as a powerful tool to help readers internalize the truth that they are never victims—only victors.

Recognizing Spiritual Battles

What are some areas where I have felt under spiritual attack?

_____
_____
_____
_____
_____
_____
_____

Identifying the Enemy's Strategies

How has the enemy tried to convince me that I am defeated?

_____
_____
_____
_____
_____
_____
_____

Standing Firm in Faith

What scriptures can I declare daily to reinforce my victory in Christ?

_____
_____
_____
_____
_____
_____
_____

Turning Setbacks into Testimonies

How has God already shown His faithfulness in past battles?

_____
_____
_____
_____
_____
_____

Embracing a Conqueror's Mindset

How can I shift my thinking from seeing myself as a victim to seeing myself as victorious?

_____
_____
_____
_____
_____
_____

Actionable Steps

Cultivate a Victory Mentality
Victory begins in the mind. Speak and think in alignment with God's Word, refusing to entertain thoughts of defeat.

Equip Yourself with Scripture
Identify key verses that reinforce your victory and memorize them. Speak them daily to counter any attack from the enemy.

Engage in Spiritual Warfare Through Praise
Praise is a weapon that enforces victory. Make it a daily habit to praise God before you see results, knowing that the battle is already won.

Personal Reflection

There is no battle that you will ever face where victory has not already been provided. The enemy is relentless in his attacks, but he is also powerless against those who refuse to believe his lies. Your faith is the key that unlocks the reality of God's promises in your life.

Choosing to walk in victory is a daily decision. It means refusing to be moved by what you see and instead standing firm on what God has said. It means using your words, your praise, and your faith as weapons against the enemy's schemes. It means recognizing that no attack is greater than the power of God working in you.

What areas of your life are you declaring victory over today? How will you stand firm in faith until you see the manifestation of God's promises? Are you willing to enforce the victory that Christ has already won for you?

_____
_____
_____
_____
_____
_____
_____
_____
_____
_____
_____
_____
_____
_____
_____
_____
_____

Closing Prayer: Lord Jesus, *I refuse to accept defeat because I know that You have already given me victory. No weapon formed against me will prosper, and every battle I face will be turned into a testimony of Your faithfulness. Strengthen me to stand firm in faith, to resist every lie of the enemy, and to walk in the full authority You have given me. Thank You for making me more than a conqueror. In Jesus' name, Amen.*

Chapter 3

...He Can't Deceive You

"And you shall know the truth, and the truth shall make you free." (John 8:32, NKJV)

There was a time in Jerry Savelle's early ministry when he found himself bombarded by doubts. The enemy whispered lies, making him question whether he was truly called to preach, whether his faith was enough, and whether God would really fulfill His promises. It was a battle in the mind—one that so many believers face daily. The enemy wasn't physically attacking him; he was attacking his perception of truth.

The devil has no real power over believers—his greatest weapon is deception. If he can make a Christian believe a lie, he can control their thoughts, actions, and even their destiny. This is why Jesus emphasized the importance of truth. The only way to break free from Satan's schemes is to replace deception with God's unshakable Word.

This battle is nothing new. From the very beginning, Satan's strategy has been to twist and distort what God says. In the Garden of Eden, he deceived Eve by questioning God's instructions: *"Has God indeed said...?"* (Genesis 3:1). His goal was to make her doubt the truth. He uses the same strategy today, trying to confuse believers about their identity, authority, and purpose.

But there is good news—the enemy cannot deceive a believer who is anchored in the truth of God's Word. Those who refuse to entertain his lies and stand on the unshakable foundation of Scripture will walk in absolute freedom. The question is, are we filling our minds with enough truth to recognize and reject deception?

Focus Point

"But the Helper, the Holy Spirit, whom the Father will send in My name, He will teach you all things, and bring to your remembrance all things that I said to you." (John 14:26, NKJV)

This verse highlights one of the greatest weapons against deception—the Holy Spirit. He is our divine teacher, leading us into all truth and exposing the lies of the enemy. The more we depend on the Spirit's guidance, the harder it becomes for Satan to manipulate our thoughts. The Holy Spirit does not merely remind us of God's Word; He empowers us to discern deception and replace it with truth.

Main Theme

The core theme of this chapter is the power of truth to dismantle deception. The enemy thrives on ignorance and confusion, but a believer who is rooted in God's Word cannot be easily shaken. Jesus emphasized that knowing the truth brings freedom because it removes Satan's ability to manipulate and control.

"Satan's greatest weapon is deception, but our greatest defense is the truth of God's Word."

Key Scriptures

- *"For Satan himself transforms himself into an angel of light."* (2 Corinthians 11:14, NKJV)
- *"My people are destroyed for lack of knowledge."* (Hosea 4:6, NKJV)
- *"Take up the whole armor of God, that you may be able to withstand in the evil day, and having done all, to stand."* (Ephesians 6:13, NKJV)

Key Points

- **The Enemy's First Strategy Is Always Deception** Before Satan attacks a believer's finances, health, or relationships, he first attacks their **belief system**. He knows that if he can control what they believe, he can control how they live.
- **Half-Truths Are Still Lies** The devil does not always present outright lies—he distorts truth just enough to make it seem reasonable. This is why discernment is crucial. Even small compromises can open the door to deception.
- **Truth Must Be Intentional** Knowing truth is not automatic. Believers must actively study and meditate on God's Word daily. The more truth they know, the more deception they will recognize.
- **Deception Leads to Bondage** Every stronghold in a believer's life begins with a lie that was accepted as truth. Breaking free starts with identifying the lie and replacing it with God's Word.
- **The Holy Spirit is the Spirit of Truth** One of the Holy Spirit's primary roles is to lead believers into all truth. Ignoring His guidance leaves room for deception to take root.
- **Armor Protects Against Lies** Ephesians 6 describes the **armor of God**, and every piece is connected to truth. Without truth, a believer is spiritually vulnerable.
- **What You Believe Determines What You Receive** Satan's goal is to make believers doubt God's promises so that they will not receive them. Faith is the key to unlocking everything God has provided.

Journaling Questions

Journaling about deception is a powerful way to recognize areas where the enemy has tried to plant lies. Writing down personal struggles, areas of doubt, and comparing them with Scripture allows believers to see the enemy's tactics clearly.

Through reflection, readers will begin to identify past deceptions, recognize how the Holy Spirit has led them into truth, and develop a strategy to remain firmly rooted in God's Word. This process is crucial in growing spiritually and ensuring that every thought aligns with truth rather than deception.

IDENTIFYING THE LIES

What are some lies the enemy has tried to make me believe about myself, God, or my purpose?

_____
_____
_____
_____
_____
_____
_____
_____

REPLACING LIES WITH TRUTH

What specific scriptures counteract the deceptions I have believed?

_____
_____
_____
_____
_____
_____
_____

DISCERNING THE ENEMY'S STRATEGIES

How has Satan used subtle half-truths to try and manipulate my faith?

_____
_____
_____
_____
_____
_____
_____

The Role of the Holy Spirit

How has the Holy Spirit revealed truth to me in the past?

_____
_____
_____
_____
_____
_____
_____

Living in Freedom

What steps can I take daily to ensure I am walking in truth and not deception?

_____
_____
_____
_____
_____
_____
_____

Actionable Steps

Cultivate a Habit of Daily Truth Intake
The only way to resist deception is by consistently feeding on God's Word. Set aside time each day to study and meditate on Scripture.

Equip Yourself with Discernment
Pray for discernment and sensitivity to the Holy Spirit. The more attuned you are to His voice, the easier it will be to recognize deception.

Engage in Bold Truth Declarations
Speak out loud what God's Word says about you. Satan's lies lose power when confronted with faith-filled declarations of truth.

Personal Reflection

Every battle we face in life is first fought in the mind. The enemy does not have the power to force us into defeat, but he works tirelessly to deceive us into surrendering what is rightfully ours. His only weapon is the lie—our only defense is truth.

Living in victory is not about struggling to defeat the enemy; it is about refusing to accept anything that contradicts what God has said. The believer who walks in truth is completely untouchable by Satan's schemes. The question is, how much truth are we feeding our minds daily?

What lies have you unknowingly accepted? What areas of your life need to be re-aligned with God's truth? Are you willing to stand firm in the Word until deception has no hold on your life?

_____
_____
_____
_____
_____
_____
_____
_____
_____
_____
_____
_____
_____
_____
_____
_____
_____
_____

Closing Prayer: *Lord Jesus, Thank You for the truth that sets me free. I refuse to be deceived by the lies of the enemy. I ask for discernment to recognize deception and wisdom to stand firm in Your Word. Holy Spirit, be my teacher and guide, leading me into all truth. I declare that I will walk in freedom, standing on the unshakable foundation of Your promises. In Jesus' name, Amen.*

Chapter 4

Satan Targets Your Dreams

"Where there is no vision, the people perish: but he that keepeth the law, happy is he." (Proverbs 29:18, KJV)

There was a time when Jerry Savelle faced a crossroads in his life. He had dreams that God had placed in his heart, yet circumstances, opinions, and the enemy's lies sought to derail them. He remembered how, as a young man, he had a deep passion for ministry, but doubts crept in: *Did God really call me? Do I have what it takes?* These questions, fueled by the enemy's tactics, threatened to extinguish the vision God had given him.

This is how Satan works—his goal is to kill dreams before they can take root. He knows that if he can stop a believer from pursuing their God-given destiny, he can limit their impact on the Kingdom. Throughout history, countless people have abandoned their dreams because they believed the lie that they were inadequate, unqualified, or incapable of fulfilling what God had spoken over their lives.

But Scripture reveals a different truth. Joseph had a dream of ruling, but before that dream was realized, he was betrayed, enslaved, and imprisoned. Everything in the natural made it seem like his dream would never come to pass. Yet, because Joseph refused to let go of what God had shown him, he stepped into his divine destiny. His story is a reminder that no attack, delay, or opposition can stop what God has ordained—unless we give up on it ourselves.

The question is, how will we respond when the enemy comes to steal our dreams? Will we surrender to fear and discouragement, or will we stand in faith, trusting that God is faithful to complete what He has started?

Focus Point

"Being confident of this very thing, that He who has begun a good work in you will complete it until the day of Jesus Christ." (Philippians 1:6, NKJV)

This verse is a powerful reminder that the dreams God gives are not fragile or easily lost. If He has started something in us, He will finish it. The enemy's job is to convince us that our dreams are too difficult, too delayed, or too impossible to accomplish. But our confidence is not in our ability—it is in God's faithfulness. No matter what obstacles arise, if we refuse to let go of the dream, we will see it come to pass.

Main Theme

The primary theme of this chapter is the enemy's relentless attack on dreams and the believer's responsibility to protect them. Every person called by God has faced opposition, yet those who persisted in faith saw their dreams fulfilled. The enemy's goal is not just to hinder progress, but to destroy vision before it produces fruit. Those who recognize his tactics and stand firm in God's promises will overcome every attack.

"The only way to lose your God-given dream is to give up on it."

Key Scriptures

- *"The thief does not come except to steal, and to kill, and to destroy. I have come that they may have life, and that they may have it more abundantly."* (John 10:10, NKJV)
- *"Delight yourself also in the Lord, and He shall give you the desires of your heart."* (Psalm 37:4, NKJV)
- *"Do not be afraid, Abram. I am your shield, your exceedingly great reward."* (Genesis 15:1, NKJV)

Key Points

- **The Enemy Attacks Vision First** Before Satan steals anything else, he tries to steal **vision**. If he can convince believers that their dreams are impossible, he can prevent them from stepping into their calling.
- **Fear is a Dream Killer** One of Satan's primary weapons is fear—fear of failure, fear of the unknown, fear of inadequacy. Those who let fear control them will never step into their full destiny.
- **Delay is Not Denial** Many believers abandon their dreams because they don't happen on their timeline. But **God's timing is perfect**, and delays are often divine setups for something greater.
- **Words Shape Destiny** The words we speak about our dreams have power. If we speak doubt and unbelief, we empower the enemy. If we speak faith, we align ourselves with God's plan.
- **Persistence Separates Those Who Succeed from Those Who Fail** Many people give up right before their breakthrough. The difference between those who fulfill their dreams and those who don't is **the refusal to quit**.
- **Dreams Must Be Guarded** Just as a farmer protects his crops from weeds and predators, believers must **protect their dreams from doubt, negativity, and discouragement**.
- **God's Promises Never Fail** If God has spoken a dream into existence, it will come to pass. The only thing that can stop it is our own decision to give up.

Journaling Questions

Journaling is a powerful tool for protecting and cultivating God-given dreams. Writing down visions, prophetic words, and personal revelations helps to anchor them in the heart. A dream that is written down is a dream that will not be easily forgotten.

Through journaling, believers can track their progress, recognize areas where the enemy has tried to discourage them, and see the faithfulness of God over time. By reflecting on past victories and lessons learned, they gain renewed confidence that what God has started, He will complete.

Recognizing the Attack

In what ways has the enemy tried to steal or discourage my God-given dreams?

_____
_____
_____
_____
_____
_____
_____

Overcoming Fear

What fears have I allowed to hinder me from fully pursuing the vision God has given me?

_____
_____
_____
_____
_____
_____

Aligning with God's Timing

How can I shift my mindset from frustration over delays to trusting God's perfect timing?

_____
_____
_____
_____
_____
_____

Speaking Life Over My Dreams

What words am I speaking over my dreams? Are they words of faith or doubt?

_____
_____
_____
_____
_____
_____

Protecting the Vision

What practical steps can I take to guard my dream from negativity and discouragement?

_____
_____
_____
_____
_____
_____

Actionable Steps

Cultivate Faith Through the Word
Find and meditate on scriptures that confirm God's plan for your life. Write them down and declare them daily.

Equip Yourself with a Vision Plan
Create a practical plan for your dream. Break it into small, actionable steps and commit to taking one step each week.

Engage in Consistent Prayer Over Your Dreams
Commit to praying over your dream daily, asking God for wisdom, direction, and divine connections to help bring it to pass.

Personal Reflection

Every great move of God began with a dream. Joseph, David, Esther, and even Jesus had a divine purpose that was opposed by the enemy, yet they refused to let go of the vision God had given them. The enemy does not attack those who have no purpose—his attacks are proof that the dream is real and worth fighting for.

The key to victory is persistence. The enemy will try to discourage, distract, and delay, but those who remain firm in faith will see their dreams fulfilled. Walking in God's calling requires not just hearing His voice, but trusting Him enough to move forward despite obstacles.

What dreams has God placed in your heart? Are you actively protecting them from the enemy's attacks? What steps will you take today to align yourself with God's plan for your life?

_____
_____
_____
_____
_____
_____
_____
_____
_____
_____
_____
_____
_____
_____
_____
_____
_____
_____
_____
_____

Closing Prayer: *Lord Jesus, I thank You for the dreams You have placed in my heart. I refuse to allow the enemy to steal, delay, or destroy them. Strengthen my faith to stand firm, even when obstacles arise. Give me wisdom to recognize deception and courage to pursue Your vision without fear. I declare that what You have started, You will finish. In Jesus' name, Amen.*

Chapter 5

It's Time to Recapture Your Dreams

"For the vision is yet for an appointed time; but at the end it shall speak, and not lie: though it tarry, wait for it; because it will surely come, it will not tarry." (Habakkuk 2:3, NKJV)

There was a time when Jerry Savelle felt that his dreams were slipping away. He had once been filled with passion and excitement about what God had called him to do, but as time passed, challenges arose, delays set in, and discouragement tried to settle in his heart. He wondered if he had missed his opportunity—if maybe the dream was no longer meant for him. It wasn't until he realized that God never cancels a calling that his faith was reignited to pursue the vision once again.

Many believers have walked through similar seasons. Life's disappointments, failures, or even distractions cause them to set aside their dreams. They begin to accept a version of life that is far less than what God originally intended for them. But the good news is that God never forgets what He placed inside of us. No matter how much time has passed, no matter how many setbacks have occurred, He is always ready to breathe new life into dreams that seem lost.

The Bible is filled with stories of people who had to recapture their dreams after moments of failure or delay. Moses fled Egypt and lived in the wilderness for 40 years before God reignited his calling. Peter denied Jesus, but Jesus restored him and reaffirmed his purpose. God's nature is redemptive—He does not disqualify those who have faced setbacks; He restores and strengthens them for the journey ahead.

The question today is not whether your dream is still possible—it is. The real question is, are you willing to rise up and recapture what God has placed inside of you?

Focus Point

"I will restore to you the years that the swarming locust has eaten..." (Joel 2:25, NKJV)

This verse is a promise of divine restoration. No matter how much time has been lost, no matter how many mistakes have been made, God is able to restore, redeem, and accelerate His plans for our lives. Satan wants believers to think that their time has run out, but God is not bound by time. He is the God of restoration, and He can accomplish in one moment what seemed impossible for years.

Main Theme

The primary theme of this chapter is the restoration of lost dreams and the courage to pursue them again. The enemy thrives on convincing believers that they have missed their opportunity, but God's Word assures us that His plans do not expire. Those who are willing to step back into faith and obedience will see dreams that seemed dead come to life again.

"The dream is not over. If God put it in your heart, He will bring it to pass."

Key Scriptures

- *"For God's gifts and His call are irrevocable."* (Romans 11:29, NKJV)
- *"Jesus said to him, 'Do not be afraid; only believe, and she will be made well.'"* (Luke 8:50, NKJV)
- *"Behold, I am the Lord, the God of all flesh. Is there anything too hard for Me?"* (Jeremiah 32:27, NKJV)

Key Points

- **The Enemy Wants You to Quit Too Soon** Many people give up right before their breakthrough. The enemy knows that if he can discourage you enough to quit, he can keep you from the fulfillment of God's plan.

- **God's Calling is Irrevocable** The gifts and callings of God are not temporary. If He has placed a dream inside you, He **never** takes it away. It is still alive, waiting for you to pursue it again.
- **Failure Does Not Cancel Destiny** Moses, Peter, and even Paul all had major failures, but God still used them mightily. Your past mistakes do not disqualify you—God's grace is greater than any failure.
- **God Can Restore Lost Time** Years may have passed, but **God is not limited by time**. He can accelerate His plans and accomplish in months what seemed impossible for decades.
- **Faith is the Key to Moving Forward** Dreams are not restored through wishful thinking—they require faith. **Believing again** is the first step to stepping into what God has prepared.
- **Obedience Opens the Door to Restoration** Many times, God gives an instruction before restoration happens. Taking steps of obedience—no matter how small—leads to the fulfillment of the dream.
- **Speaking Life Over Your Dreams is Essential** Words have power. Begin to declare what God has said about your dreams instead of focusing on past disappointments.

Journaling Questions

Journaling about dreams is a powerful way to bring clarity and direction. Many people have dreams buried deep within them but have never written them down. When you write the vision, you begin to take ownership of it (Habakkuk 2:2).

By journaling, readers will uncover areas where discouragement may have crept in, identify fears that have held them back, and begin to align their thoughts with God's promises. Writing out past victories will also serve as a reminder that if God has been faithful before, He will be faithful again.

Rediscovering the Dream

What dreams has God placed in my heart that I have set aside or forgotten?

_____
_____
_____

Breaking Free from Fear

What fears or doubts have prevented me from pursuing my God-given dream?

_____
_____
_____
_____
_____
_____

Aligning with God's Timing

How can I begin trusting that God's timing is perfect for my life?

_____
_____
_____
_____
_____
_____

Speaking Life Over My Future

What declarations can I begin making over my dreams to reinforce my faith?

_____
_____
_____
_____
_____
_____

Taking the First Step

What is one practical step I can take this week to begin pursuing my dream again?

_____
_____
_____
_____
_____
_____

Actionable Steps

Cultivate a Vision Mindset
Start each day by **visualizing** the dream God has placed inside of you. Meditate on scriptures that align with your calling and purpose.

Equip Yourself with a Faith Strategy
Develop a **written plan** for pursuing your dream. Set goals, identify obstacles, and commit to taking action in faith.

Engage in Bold Obedience
Be willing to take **immediate steps of obedience**. Even if the full vision is not clear, trust God enough to move forward.

Personal Reflection

The enemy wants nothing more than to convince believers that their dreams are over. He whispers lies that it's too late, too hard, or too impossible. But the truth is, if God placed the dream in your heart, it is still alive. The only way to fail is to stop pursuing what God has called you to do.

Your journey is not about how many setbacks you have faced—it is about whether or not you will keep moving forward. The difference between those who see their dreams fulfilled and those who don't is persistence. God is waiting for you to take that first step.

Will you choose to believe again? Will you stand in faith and reclaim what God has promised? Are you ready to recapture your dream and walk boldly into your destiny?

___

Closing Prayer: Lord Jesus,

I thank You that my dreams are not lost. I choose today to recapture what You have placed inside of me. I refuse to believe the lies of the enemy that it is too late or too hard. You are the God of restoration, and I trust that You will bring to completion everything You have started in my life. Give me the courage to step out in faith and pursue what You have called me to do. In Jesus' name, Amen.

About the Author

Dr. Jerry Savelle was an average, blue-collar man who struggled and needed God's help. While he considered himself a "nobody," when he became a believer, God told him not to worry about it because He was a master at making champions out of nobodies. God took Dr. Savelle from being a constant quitter to a man who knew how to stand on the Word of God until victory was experienced. Because of the life-changing combination of God's faithfulness and Dr. Savelle's "no quit" attitude, his life was totally different than it was fifty years ago.

Since 1969, Dr. Savelle traveled the world, teaching people how to win in life. Dr. Savelle ministered in over thirty-five hundred churches in over forty nations and had overseas offices in the United Kingdom, Australia, Canada, and South Africa, as well as numerous Bible Schools in several nations.

God used Dr. Savelle to inspire people worldwide to take hold of the promises of God and become the winners in life that God has called them to be, and to become a testimony to His faithfulness.

He hosted the Jerry Savelle Ministries television broadcast in two hundred countries worldwide. He was the author of more than seventy books, including his bestsellers: If Satan Can't Steal Your Joy, He Can't Keep Your Goods and Called to Battle, Destined to Win. He and his wife, Carolyn, also served as founding pastors of Heritage of Faith Christian Center in Crowley, Texas.

Harrison House is a Spirit-filled, Word of Faith Christian publisher dedicated to spreading the message of faith, hope, and love through our wide range of inspiring publications. Committed to the messages that highlight the power of the Word and Spirit, we provide books, devotionals, and study guides that empower believers to live victorious, faith-filled lives.

Our resources are designed to help readers grow spiritually, strengthen their faith, and experience the transformative power of God's Word. Harrison House is passionate about equipping Christians with the tools they need to fulfill their divine purpose and impact the world for Christ.

www.ingramcontent.com/pod-product-compliance
Lightning Source LLC
Chambersburg PA
CBHW080913170426
43201CB00017B/2316